Z
49
.A1
C35
1986

Cassingham, R. C.
(Randy C.)

The Dvorak keyboard

DATE		

**BUSINESS/SCIENCE/TECHNOLOGY
DIVISION**

The Dvorak Keyboard

The Ergonomically Designed
Typewriter Keyboard,
Now an American Standard

by

R. C. Cassingham

Freelance Communications
Arcata, California

Z
49
. A1
C35
1986

Published by Freelance Communications,
Post Office Box 717, Arcata CA 95521.

Printed and bound in the United States of America

International Standard Book Number (ISBN): 0-935309-10-1
Library of Congress Catalog Card Number: 85-81287

August Dvorak, PhD.
May 5, 1894–October 10, 1975

Acknowledgements

Rarely can one person take all the credit for putting together a book. I gratefully acknowledge the help of many persons, including:

Belmont Adams and **Phil Davis**, long-time Dvorak devotees, who provided quite a bit of raw materials, including difficult-to-find copies of many of the studies quoted in this book;

Freelance writers and friends **Lindsey McWilliams** and **Bob Nelson**, and my father **Larry Cassingham**, for editing help;

Virginia Russell, president of the Dvorak International Federation, for giving the manuscript "one last look" to double check for technical accuracy;

And **Hermione Dvorak**, Dr. August Dvorak's widow, who supplied historical information on the genesis of the Dvorak Simplified Keyboard.

Thank you,

Randy Cassingham
Arcata, California
December, 1985

CONTENTS

The United States has pressed blindly on for over a century
with a terrible keyboard. It is time to change to a better one.

The "Standard" keyboard that we use today – known as
Qwerty – was designed to work around mechanical limitations
that no longer exist. It is an inefficient, wasteful layout we could
well do without.

The Simplified Keyboard, as it was first known, was
designed for maximum efficiency and, significantly, comfort
for the typist. It has been refined over its life, and is now
becomming quite popular.

More than 40 years ago, the U.S. Navy studied the Dvorak
keyboard hoping to help alleviate the shortage of typists during
the war years. The study clearly shows the superiority of the
rational layout, but the report was inexplicably classified for
many years and made unavailable to the public.

Foreword

Since 1872, typists have used a keyboard that was designed to slow their speed. In 1936 a keyboard was patented that was easier to learn. Because of the arrangement of keys on the Dvorak keyboard, the operator experienced less fatigue, less errors, and more speed.

Until the computer revolution, hardware conversion from the Qwerty keyboard to the Dvorak keyboard was difficult. With the technology today, the problem of conversion from one keyboard to the other no longer exists.

The task of studying typewriter behavior and evaluating keyboard efficiency has been taken on by many researchers in the past. The majority of these keyboard engineers had the motivation to search for the optimal arrangement of letters on the keyboard. The results of the research have consistently emphasized the disadvantages of the Qwerty keyboard.

The most ambitious attempt to unseat the Qwerty keyboard was begun by August Dvorak, a professor of education at the University of Washington, and his brother-in-law, William Dealey. Dvorak and Dealey had long been admirers of industrial engineers Frank and Lillian Gilbreth. The Gilbreths advocated the reduction of worker fatigue by the elimination of wasted motion. The typewriter keyboard was a part of the Gilbreths' motion and time studies.

With the introduction of computers and acceptance of the Dvorak keyboard by the American National Standards Institute in November 1982, the Dvorak has finally begun to receive the recognition it deserves. In the years in which I have been involved with the Dvorak keyboard, I have also seen the computer become an accepted device within the office. The computer and the Dvorak have grown up together within the business world. There are many users of computers who have never typed. It is that population that has realized that learning a keyboard designed for touch typing makes sense over a keyboard designed for hunt-and-peck.

I agree with the experts in the industry who predict that within two years, there will be as many Dvorak keyboards sold as Qwerty.

The Dvorak Keyboard has been written at a critical time in the history of the Dvorak keyboard. I believe that this book will help to answer the basic questions frequently asked about the Dvorak keyboard.

It is impossible to give due credit to all the people who have promoted the Dvorak keyboard. Rather than omit anyone, I'm sending a blanket thank-you to everyone who has helped the Dvorak keyboard to become accepted. You know who you are. As in any endeavor, there are many unsung heros.

Virginia de Ganahl Russell
President, Dvorak International Federation
Brandon, Vermont
December, 1985

Chapter One

Introduction

"With the fierce international trade competition, the West has only a small price to pay to stay competitive in industrial productivity: switching to a more efficient keyboard." – Dr. Hisao Yamada, University of Toyko.

The quote by Hisao Yamada at the beginning of this chapter, taken by itself, seems an absurd exaggeration. But it is the kind of statement intelligent, informed people make time and time again when they talk about the Dvorak keyboard. The Dvorak will increase productivity for very little conversion cost and after trying it, typists like it better.

If you supervise a word processing center, type for a living, use a computer or a typewriter, do not hesitate to leave behind the archaic keyboard known as "Qwerty". Why stick with a keyboard that makes typing slow, awkward and inefficient when an effective alternative is readily available?

The Dvorak (pronounced "duh-VOR-ack") keyboard was designed in the 1930s by Dr. August Dvorak, a professor of education and psychology at the University of Washington (and a distant cousin of the Czech composer Anton Dvorak). His design is simply a rearrangement of the keys for a typewriter or computer keyboard.

The ANSI standard Dvorak layout.
Blank keys are for optional graphic characters.

The *de facto* standard "Qwerty" keyboard was **designed** specifically to be inefficient because of the mechanical limitations of early typewriters. Since its introduction in 1873,

Qwerty has remained the primary keyboard in use throughout the English-speaking world – not because it was considered good but because it became entrenched in tradition.

Regardless of that tradition, the Dvorak layout has persisted; there has always been someone taking advantage of its superiority over the Qwerty layout. It resurfaces as a hot topic in the popular press again and again. Arguments against its adoption have kept the Dvorak out of the mainstream for some time (see Chapter 5), but those arguments are generally no longer valid. The Dvorak keyboard is catching on at a rapid rate, thanks in part to its being accepted as the "alternate standard" by the American National Standards Institute in November, 1982.

Insurance companies, which deal with enormous amounts of paperwork, have been the first to switch to the Dvorak. State Farm, Aetna and many others have pilot programs in progress, and the results are very encouraging. American Telephone and Telegraph has installed 14,000 terminals with Dvorak keyboards into their directory assistance centers, where time *really* means money. And governmental offices, both state and federal, are using it to save the taxpayers' money.

How much better is Dvorak than Qwerty? Dr. Dvorak, who died in 1975, showed with slow motion films that in an eight-hour day, a full-time typist's fingers travel between 12 and 20 *MILES*. Using the Dvorak keyboard on the same text, the finger travel is only *one* mile. The Dvorak design is faster, easier to use, more productive and less stressful for the typist.

And the Dvorak is even easier to learn. Sixth graders can type 40 words per minute on the Dvorak after only a few weeks of training. An adult typically gets to 40 WPM in 18 hours of training; it takes more than three times as long (56 hours) to reach that skill level on the Qwerty.

Barbara Blackburn was in a Qwerty typing class in high

school; she flunked out. Today, using the Dvorak keyboard, she holds the title as one of the fastest typists in the world. She can type at over *two hundred* words per minute -- that's more than double the speed of a good executive secretary.

One educator estimated that implementation of the Dvorak in American businesses would save millions of dollars per year. Not only would production increase, but the reduction of stress and fatigue could reduce workers' stress related illnesses.

The president of the Dvorak International Federation, a member-funded information organization, estimated that in 1974 there were 2,000 typists using the Dvorak. At the end of 1984, she estimated there were over 100,000 users. The Dvorak is on its way.

It is easy to switch; Dvorak-equipped machines are available right now. There are replacement keyboards and conversion programs for computers on the market that will change almost any computer's keyboard to Dvorak with a keystroke. And computer-based tutorials make the retraining easy.

The ANSI Qwerty keyboard layout.

What, exactly, makes Qwerty – currently the primary keyboard in use today – so bad that we should abandon it? Dr. Dvorak pointed out the several characteristics that make the Qwerty layout unacceptable for modern use:

1) Many of the letter sequences (common combinations of letters) typed on Qwerty require awkward finger motions. These motions are tiring and make typing prone to errors.

2) Many of these sequences are typed with the same finger, slowing down typing and putting an unnecessary burden on the weaker fingers.

3) Many of these sequences are stroked on different rows while jumping over the "home" row where the fingers normally rest. This slows the typist and increases fatigue.

4) Many of the sequences are on the same hand, while the other sits idle. Alternating between the hands makes typing faster and easier.

5) A high number of sequences are struck by the left hand, which is usually the weaker hand.

6) Many sequences are struck with adjacent fingers, which is slower than using other fingers.

7) Thirty percent of the sequences on Qwerty involve the lower row, which is the slowest and most difficult row to hit.

8) Eighty percent of the sequences involve the upper row, an excessive amount that needlessly reduces speed and efficiency.

9) Only about 51 percent of the sequences use the home row, where the fingers are normally supposed to rest.

10) The arrangement of the Qwerty keys is not optimized for the physiology of the human hand or the structure of written language.

Could the Qwerty layout be worse? Not much. Dr. Dvorak once said that you could probably design a better layout by mixing the letters of the alphabet in a hat and then putting them on the keyboard at random.

In the chapters that follow, the failings of the Qwerty are explored in more depth. The logical design and the benefits of the Dvorak layout are presented. And the reasons why it took until now to be widely accepted in America are discussed. There is also a chapter that will help you to convert from Qwerty to Dvorak, and an Appendix lists many of the products available which support the keyboard. In a world where computers and word processors are a part of everyday life, and where employee stress and comfort have become important considerations in the workplace, the Dvorak keyboard, long known to be superior in speed, comfort and productivity, makes more sense than ever.

Chapter 2

The Qwerty Keyboard

"Every typist should curse the name of Christopher Latham Sholes." – Jim Ritter, writer.

Christopher Latham Sholes, the inventor of the first practical typewriter, struggled with a problem: even when typists tapped the keys on his machine slowly, the sluggish action of the type bars made the typewriter jam often. Sholes experimented with moving the keys around to slow down the typists in hopes of eliminating the jamming. The keyboard he eventually developed is still used on typewriters today with very few alterations. Later dubbed the "Qwerty" keyboard because of the arrangement of the keys on the top row, it is also the "standard" keyboard found on most computers today.

Sholes didn't invent the typewriter – 51 inventors from several different countries were issued patents for typewriters before him – but none were practical for mass manufacturing and use. Even Thomas Edison got into the act by saying several times that he helped build the Sholes typewriter, a claim repeated in his biography. Edison apparently had been trying to build a workable typewriter but without much success. Objective records show that he had no tie to Sholes during that time, so few take his claim seriously.

One of Sholes' biggest problems in getting his machine to work was the keyboard layout. He started with an alphabetic arrangement, then moved keys randomly to reduce jamming. Later, Sholes obtained a list of the most common letters used in English. Armed with this list, Sholes radically altered his original alphabetical arrangement.

He used the list to spread the most-used letters away from each other, making the jumps between the letters – sequences – harder and slower to strike. It was Sholes' intention to slow down typists with Qwerty, and it was this layout that Remington Arms company used when the first commercial machine hit the market in 1873. We have used his 19th Century typist-slowing keyboard almost exclusively since.

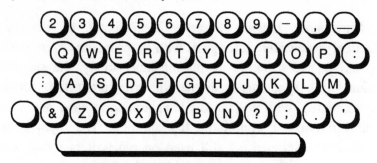

The original Qwerty layout from the first
Sholes-designed Remington typewriter

Although some individuals have contested the idea, historians and researchers agree that Sholes indeed meant to slow down typists, who in those days typed with two fingers. And Qwerty *did* bring key-jamming down to an acceptable level as Sholes wanted. When he first conceived of his "type-writing machine", as Sholes called it, he intended typing to match the speed of handwriting, which is generally below 20 words per minute. The new keyboard allowed typing to proceed with a minimum of jamming, and resulted in the first marketable typewriter.

But even then, the keyboard layout wasn't immediately accepted. "Index" typewriters, where a letter was typed by dialing a pointer to the desired letter and pulling a handle, were in much more demand for quite a while after Sholes' type-writer came on the market. They were quite popular for over a decade, but died out when ten-finger typing proved a superior method.

Touch Typing

Ten-finger typing was unheard of in those early days; people seldom typed with more than one or two fingers, rarely three or four, all the while staring intently at the keyboard, finding the key they wanted to strike by sight. Later, this system was dubbed the "Columbus system" because a "discovery" was necessary for each key that was struck. Today, it is better known as the "hunt-and-peck" system.

Around 1878, two-finger typing started to die out, making way for a new method promoted by Mrs. L. V. Longley, the head of a stenographic school in Cincinnati. She was the first to declare publicly that all 10 fingers should be used for typing.

The public response was swift: contempt and derision. Typewriting journals, which were popular at the time, ran editorials condemning the use of the "weak" little and ring fingers.

Then, Frank E. McGurrin, a Federal Court clerk in Salt Lake City, developed a system of typing using all of his fingers *without* looking at the keys. Because of his confidence in his method, he proclaimed himself the world's fastest typist, which angered a Cincinnati man named Louis Taub, who had already made the same claim.

On July 25, 1888, the first typing contest was held to determine which, McGurrin or Taub, was the fastest. McGurrin's ten-finger typing won easily over Taub, who used four fingers and looked at the keys when he typed. (Women didn't compete in these first speed contests because there were very few female secretaries in those days. But they broke into office work shortly thereafter when the YWCA started teaching typing to women. The women who graduated were employed quickly due to a shortage of typists. Many credit the typewriter for opening the doors of business to women -- or, conversely, for subjecting them to 100 years of stenographic slavery.)

After several speed contests had proven its superiority, "touch" typing was no longer held in contempt but so amazed people that it caught on rapidly. The term "touch," incidentally, was introduced in 1889 by the author of the first typing manual to teach the system. It is because we use the touch method, a method that Sholes clearly did not anticipate when he designed the Qwerty, that we should now drop the old layout in favor of the Dvorak, which *was* designed for touch typing.

Qwerty and Touch Typing

Most typists are right handed, but in touch typing, the Qwerty keyboard forces the weaker left hand to do almost 58 percent of the work. In addition, the "finger loads" -- the amount of typing done with each finger -- is far from even or properly distributed in regard to each finger's strength and skill. The index fingers of each hand perform more than 44 percent of the strokes on the Qwerty layout. Worse, only 32 percent of the strokes are on the "home" row where the fingers normally rest; 52 percent are done on the upper row.

Still worse is the number of awkward sequences on the Qwerty keyboard. The English language has a limited number of sequences. Dvorak studied the language extensively, and made a list of the sequences, or "digraphs", that make up written text. A digraph, as Dvorak defined it, is a sequence of two letters that make a single sound when spoken. The number of digraphs used in English is smaller than one might imagine – far less than just a list of random two-letter combinations (we don't use most combinations at all, such as q-k).

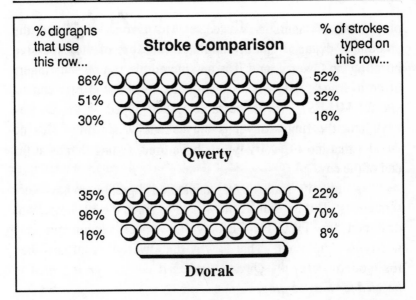

Of the number of digraphs that do make up the English language (and this generally applies to all languages that use our alphabet), about 137 digraphs, (such as e-d, a-s, t-e, etc.), make up 90 percent of typewritten text. The eleven most common digraphs account for one-quarter, 34 make up one-half, and just 57 digraphs account for three-quarters of all typewritten copy.

On the Qwerty keyboard, almost half of these common digraphs are keyed with the same hand and sometimes with the same finger, such as the common e-d. The consequence of this is that these common strokes are much more difficult to type than necessary – obviously an inefficient practice – and errors are far more likely to occur as the difficulty rises.

The worst problem by far, however, is the enormous amount of "hurdling" necessary on the Qwerty layout. One finger often jumps, or hurdles, back and forth from row to row, sometimes never touching on the home row, during typing. An example of this is the word "minimum". The first finger on the right hand does all the typing while the potential of the other fingers is wasted.   Dr. Dvorak measured the amount of distance that accumulated because of the excessive hurdling on Qwerty, and it is an incredible figure: the fingers of an average typist who types all day will travel between 12 and 20 *MILES!* But if the same text is typed on the Dvorak keyboard, the finger travel is only about *ONE* mile. It's no wonder that most Qwerty typists have tired, aching hands at the end of the day.

It is unlikely Sholes ever considered digraphs or any other sequences. But he didn't really have to since the keyboard was designed for TWO-FINGER typing where sequencing isn't nearly as important. That is why the Qwerty layout is so bad for modern use: *the Qwerty keyboard was **never** intended to be used for touch typing.*

✦ Dr. Dvorak certainly wasn't the first to see the inherent weakness of the Qwerty layout. "It is needless to say that the weakness of the Qwerty keyboard was immediately recognized by almost anyone who had ever taken a hard look at the keyboard," writes Hisao Yamada, a Japanese scholar studying the evolution of typewriting in the West.

The Japanese did not have a suitable touch typing system or even a standard keyboard until recently because their language needs a keyboard with hundreds of characters. Yamada helped to make standard an ergonomic keyboard for the Japanese language that starts out with a logical, useful design.

"The reason of such intensive examination (of the Qwerty keyboard) on our part is to learn from a predecessor's experience the degree of suffering we must be prepared to encounter if we are careless at the onset," he wrote. "If we make a similar error (as the West) for the lack of careful study now, we would not be able to excuse ourselves."

Yamada's study of the Qwerty keyboard paid off: after a successful touch keyboard design was implemented in Japan, he was asked to come to China to design one there.

It is easy to say the Qwerty layout is bad, and it is also easy to improve upon it. But it is not easy to decide on the "best" layout. There is an enormous number of possible layouts for the 26 letters, the period, comma, apostrophe and hyphen. Even only using these 30 keys, there are *265,000,000,000, 000,000,000,000,000,000,000 possible layouts.* (That's 2.65 times 10^{32} or 265 trillion quadrillions, a number that defies comprehension.)

Many inventors worked on improved keyboard layouts, starting with Sholes himself. As early as 1896, Sholes was granted a patent for an improved typewriter. One of his improvements was a keyboard which concentrated the vowels on the home row in much the same manner as on the Dvorak keyboard. That keyboard was only one of about 200 designs that have been patented since Qwerty.

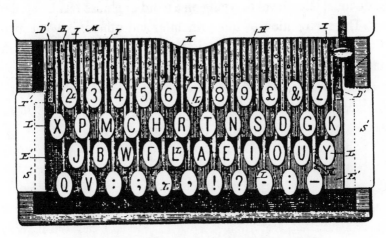

Sholes Improved keyboard, designed in 1889.

But Sholes, and probably all the keyboard designers that followed him until Dvorak, neglected the most important design consideration: the relation keys had to one another. Since touch typing wasn't even thought of for many years, typing was long considered from the sole aspect of one letter at a time. Touch typists work in sequences that are sometimes many words long. Words are struck as wholes by experienced typists, and they typically are not consciously aware of the individual letters.

Typing is much like reading. Right now, are you reading words and phrases, or are you looking at individual letters, then forming them into words, then phrases, then deciding what they mean? If so, you are a very slow reader. Typists who work on the level of one letter at a time are likewise very slow, and that method of typing isn't what is meant by "typewriting". It is the placement of sequences necessary to make words and phrases that makes typing on the Qwerty keyboard, and the other keyboards that followed, awkward and difficult. Typewriting goes much faster when the typist can make the jump from the individual letter level to typing on a word or phrase level.

The recognition of this principle, and others, is what made the Dvorak keyboard an important leap forward in the technology of keyboard design.

Chapter 3

The Dvorak Keyboard

⚹ "Fitting machines to people is cheaper and easier than fitting people to machines." – Frank Gilbreth, Industrial Engineer and pioneer of ergonomics.

Dvorak didn't name the new keyboard after himself; he referred to it as the "Simplified Keyboard", a name that reflected the intention of its design. It wasn't until some time later that the keyboard was referred to as "The Dvorak Keyboard".

The Dvorak Simplified Keyboard, or DSK, was the name most often used until the early 1980s. It now refers mainly to Dvorak's original design, which is recognizable by its unique numeral order on the top row (see diagrams). When the Smith-Corona typewriter company modified that original design and marketed their simplified typewriter in the 1970s, they put the digits back into numerical order and dubbed it the "American Simplified Keyboard" or ASK.

After some further refinements, the keyboard was adopted as the "alternate" standard by the American National Standards Institute (ANSI). That specific keyboard design is usually just called "The Dvorak Keyboard" to signify the differences from the original design and the variations that followed. But whatever it is called, it remains the most tested replacement for the Qwerty keyboard, and it is the most logical and economical route to improve typist productivity and comfort.

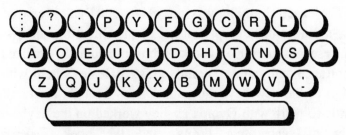

Dvorak and dealey's original simplified keyboard design from their 1932 patent specification. Number order was not specified.

⊬ Doctors Frank and Lillian Gilbreth, a husband and wife team, excelled in the science of motion and time study at the turn of the century. ⟨They were pioneers in the field of "ergonomics" – the study of the interaction between humans and machines and the effects that machines have on humans. As a part of their studies, they made slow motion films of expert typists at work.

⋇ Dr. August Dvorak, who was an educational psychologist and professor of education at Washington State University, became interested in keyboard design when Gertrude Ford, a teacher from Grove City College (Pennsylvania) came to the University of Washington for a summer session to write a Master's thesis on typing errors.

Ford was interested in why the most commonly mispelled words on a typewriter were very simple words, such as "the". She selected Dr. Dvorak as her major adviser, and he also became interested in the typewriter. After study of the keyboard, he concluded a complete revision of its layout would be needed.

Dr. William Dealey, Dvorak's brother-in-law, was an excellent typist, having subscribed to one of the early touch typing correspondence courses. In the summers of 1914 and 1915, Dealey attended seminars in scientific motion study conducted by the Gilbreths.

The exact chronology is not clear, but Dealey viewed the slow-motion films of typists made by the Gilbreths, and brought this research to Dr. Dvorak, who immediately realized its importance and value. Dvorak enlisted Dealey's help with the design of the new keyboard, and Dealey brought his family to Seattle to work with Dvorak as they worked on the keyboard, a study of typewriting errors, and the book *Typewriting Behavior*. Gertrude Ford also worked on that book, as did Nellie Merrick, a research assistant to the Carnegie Foundation for the Advancement of Teaching Study of Typewriting and the director of personal typing at the Tacoma (Washington) public schools. The process took more than a decade.

The *Typewriting Behavior* book was often called "the report to the Carnegie Foundation" in response to that foundation's two grants totalling $14,000 for the study of typewriting. It has often been assumed that the grants funded the research for the design of the simplified keyboard, but the keyboard design had already been finished by the time the grants were made. Some of the grant money probably was used, though, to study the teaching effectiveness of using the new simplified keyboard versus the Qwerty.

During the simplified keyboard's design phase, one of the limitations Dvorak and Dealey imposed on themselves was that they didn't want to alter the physical structure of the typewriter. They designed it to be easy and cheap to alter existing machines and to manufacture typewriters with an easier-to-use keyboard without having to alter the manufacturing process significantly. This showed considerable foresight – as we have seen from history of keyboards, it is difficult enough to make a change without having to scrap all existing equipment.

While working on the design, Dvorak and Dealey studied the English language extensively, making charts of the most used letters and combinations of letters by counting letters from printed text and conversations. They studied the physiology of the hand and researched the many different designs proposed for keyboards in the past, analyzing all that came their way.

Earlier designers of keyboards had not considered the importance of the keyboard design as a whole. They didn't realize that how the keys are placed determines how sequences are stroked. Dvorak and Dealey discovered that the ease or difficulty of striking these sequences makes typing easy and fast, or awkward, slow, and error prone.

The "classic" Dvorak design, as shown in the 1936 book Typewriting Behavior. Note the order of the numerals.

As mentioned in chapter two, it was Dvorak and Dealey's attention to digraphs (the two-letter sequence that makes a single sound) that helps make the Dvorak layout so simple to learn and use. It is simpler than might be expected to design a keyboard to stroke common digraphs, mostly because of the small number of them used to make up the English language.

Dvorak and Dealey also had several other objectives when they designed their keyboard. Their first was to plan the layout scientifically to decrease the likelihood of error, which would help to increase speed and lessen the fatigue of typing. They wanted to make typing less awkward by simplifying the stroking of common letter sequences, which also would help to lessen errors. And they wanted to make typing more rhythmic by making the strokes alternate as much as possible between the hands, which also helps increase speed, reduce errors and reduce fatigue.

The way the human hand is structured also figured into the design of the simplified layout. For instance, the Dvorak keyboard is optimized for "inboard stroke flow". When fingers on the same hand must do stroking in succession, the little

finger (or   another "outside finger") does the first stroke
followed by a stroke from a finger closer to the thumb. This is
easier than going the other way. For an example of this, drum
your fingers on a tabletop. It is more comfortable for most
when they start with their little finger and proceed to the
thumb. For an example of how this works on the Dvorak, try
the word "stay".

Taking such subtle aspects as inboard stroke flow into
consideration shows the effort that went into the design of the
Dvorak layout. Inboard stroke flow doesn't add an enormous
amount to the productivity of the typist – though it does help
some – yet it does show the lengths Dvorak and Dealey went to
to make typing easier and less fatiguing.

Dr. Dvorak was almost obsessed with the comfort of the
typist.   In *Typewriting Behavior*, for example, there were
several discussions on how typists should properly relax, how
they should be in comfortable, adjustable chairs with adjustable
tables – factors which would be considered simple ergonomics
today. It was Dvorak's goal to make typing easier and less
stressful.

The original Dvorak design has been refined a bit over the
years. The first publicly released simplified layout didn't have
a lot of detail – the order of the numbers, for instance, wasn't
specified, as they were later. The design was released in 1932,
when Dvorak and Dealey applied for their first keyboard patent.

When *Typewriting Behavior* was published in 1936, the
simplified keyboard was a bit more refined. For instance, the
book showed a number order that was different than numeric –
their locations based instead on frequency of use.

Over the next 45 years, there were minor changes made to
the layout. Mostly, the symbols were moved about (such as the
slash, question mark, colon and semi-colon, and quote marks).

As often-used characters, the period and comma always remained in the same place on the upper row; the letters also remained in almost the exact original positions.

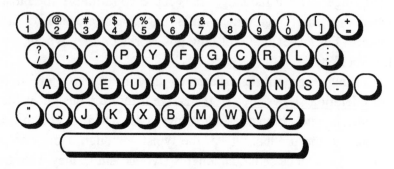

The "American Simplified Keyboard", or ASK, that the Smith-Corona typewriter company introduced in 1975.

The uncontrolled shifting of these keys caused some slight problems. By the end of the 1970s, there was a debate on exactly where the symbol keys should go, and whether the numbers should be in numeric or "classic Dvorak" order. Pushed into action by proponents of the Dvorak layout, the American National Standards Institute (ANSI) convened a technical committee to decide. Later, the technical committee made its recommendation to ANSI and the draft proposal for a new standard went to the ANSI Committee on Information Processing Systems ("X3"), made up of representatives of many large American businesses and governmental agencies, among them Control Data Corp., Digital Equipment Corp., Hewlett-Packard, IBM, Wang, Xerox, the U.S. General Services Administration, the National Bureau of Standards, and the departments of Defense and Justice.

All of these companies didn't necessarily approve of the design, but the standard for the Dvorak keyboard was approved on November 19, 1982. Now known as ANSI X4.22-1983, the standard gave a respectability to the Dvorak keyboard that it really hadn't seen before: official recognition as an "alternate" layout for alphanumeric keyboards.

The ANSI standard Dvorak layout X4.22-1983.

The flurry of publicity that followed the adoption of the standard gave new life to the keyboard. Manufacturers didn't have to suffer through the several different versions (such as different number order styles) when deciding on keyboard layout. Before the ANSI standard was adopted, the Dvorak International Federation estimated there were about 5,000 people who used the Dvorak keyboard. But DIF estimated over 100,000 people were using it by the end of 1984.

Because of the new standard, computer manufacturers started making the Dvorak layout available on their keyboards. Apple Computer's IIc model was the first personal computer to have a switch right on it that allows the user to choose between the Qwerty and Dvorak keyboards.

Now, many companies offer products which make it possible to, at any time, switch between Dvorak and Qwerty on most any computer. So companies can hire Dvorak trained operators without having to junk their existing equipment. If a typist comes along who only knows Qwerty, they can flip the switch and have it. With such a choice, the last major obstacle to the implementation of the Dvorak keyboard on a widespread basis has passed. Now, all that is needed is the presentation of proof from an objective comparative experiment that the Dvorak actually does increase productivity, and that the productivity is significant enough to warrant a changeover.

Chapter 4

The Navy Study

"There is little need to demonstrate further the superiority of the Dvorak keyboard in experimental tests. Plenty of well-documented evidence exists." – S. N. Alexander, Chief, Information Technology Division, U.S. National Bureau of Standards.

During World War II, the U.S. Navy studied the Dvorak keyboard and presented their findings in a detailed report ("A Practical Experiment in Simplified Keyboard Retraining", July 1944). It was one of the earliest comprehensive, objective, independent experiments made on the keyboard. It pitted the Qwerty keyboard against the then fairly new Dvorak Simplified layout, and the methods and results were carefully recorded. The results were astounding.

Dr. Dvorak was a Commander in the Navy reserve during the time of the experiment, but he did not call for the test nor did he participate in any way, as many have assumed. Some went so far as to suggest that the experiment must have been very biased because of Dvorak's input. It is likely that he didn't participate in the test to avoid just this sort of objection. His only contribution was to supply the typewriters from his personal stock for use in the test. During the war, typewriters were scarce, so it was hard to justify taking working machines out of production for an experiment.

The Navy – and the rest of the government – had a genuine interest in increasing their typists' productivity. During the 1940s, there was a significant shortage of trained typists. Few typists could match the skill that supposedly was required to work for the government. Competence, according to U.S. Civil Service Commission standards prior to 1941, required, in part, that a typist be able to type at 50 net words per minute for 10 to 15 minutes. However, as the Navy's researchers pointed out, studies showed that after *three years* of typing instruction, the average typing student's speed was only 47 net words per minute (NWPM -- the gross speed as measured for a ten-minute period minus the number of errors made). Those student's overall gain in NWPM per hour of instruction was only .09 for those three years.

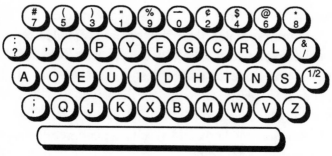

The Navy used the "classic" Dvorak layout for their study, but the results should apply to the newer ANSI version of the Dvorak as well.

For the Navy's study, 14 typists were retrained from the Qwerty keyboard to the Dvorak to see if retraining was feasible, if conversion would be profitable, and to determine what type of retraining method was best. Results were shown quickly: "their average typing speed on the 13th day (at less than two hours of retraining per day) was 21 NWPM or 64 percent of their Standard Keyboard rate," the report said. The average time required for the typists to reach their "standard" (Qwerty) keyboard net speed was 52 hours. The average NWPM per hour of retraining was .70 (contrast that to the average gain of .09 NWPM per hour for the average typists' initial training). The subjects' net typing scores were on average 93 percent faster on the Dvorak keyboard than on Qwerty.

Ease of training doesn't necessarily affect productivity. But the final results showed the experimental subjects increased their accuracy by an average of 68 percent, and the average net increase over their Qwerty keyboard typing speed was 74 percent, the best increase was 244 percent. The combination of the increased accuracy and speed significantly increased the typists' productivity. "Indisputably," the report said, "it is obvious that The Simplified Keyboard is easier to master than the Standard Keyboard."

In a retraining effort, the report said, expect the following: "After 100 hours of retraining on the Simplified Keyboard the group average should be (70 NWPM). Whereas 100 hours of additional training on the Standard Keyboard with a similar group would give an average of about (48 NWPM). The comparison... could be 70 to 48, or 146 percent, in the Simplified Keyboard's favor." (Modern retraining efforts, using computer-based tutorials, have nearly chopped that retraining time in half.)

Would there have been a similar increase in speed and productivity if Standard Keyboard training was given to these typists instead of Simplified Keyboard training? Since the standard keyboard has such terrible limitations (i.e., the poor layout), "continuation or additional training cannot be expected to produce more improvement in net speed per hour of instruction than was secured from initial training on the same Standard Keyboard." In other words, *no*.

Was the retraining "profitable"? Very. It only took 10.3 *days* for the typist's increased productivity to pay for the net cost of retraining, and that included the cost of machine conversion! "These 14 retrained typists are capable of turning out as much typewritten work as 27 typists with the average ability possessed by this group on the Standard Keyboard (before retraining)," the report said. "To turn out on the Standard Keyboard the additional amount of work would, therefore, require 13 additional typists, 13 additional type-writers, 13 additional desks and chairs, and enough space for (them)." Also, "in an emergency the best practical results in the shortest time will be secured on the Simplified Keyboard by retraining the poorer Standard Keyboard typists."

The gain wouldn't really be profitable, though, if the effects of the training wore off as soon as the training period ended. So the experimenters returned and tested the typists again two months later. "The results of the retesting showed that some of the typists had actually increased their Simplified Keyboard typing speed while on the job," the report said. "The average of all the typists' retest scores showed that the group had retained the high net typing speed gained in the 83-hour retraining class. This is in contrast to the results familiar to employers of Standard Keyboard typists whose typing speed and production rates rarely equal their final class test scores and *frequently suffer decreases of 50 percent or more*" (emphasis from original).

In addition, the researchers asked the typists for their reactions to their retraining. They "were unanimous in their approval of the Simplified Keyboard," the experimenters reported. They found it easy to learn, more accurate, less fatiguing, and easier and more enjoyable to type on. It produced less tension and strain, and the typists found that their newly increased typing productivity left time for other necessary work. They also reported getting better pay and bonuses because of their greater productivity.

The typists made these comments about the Dvorak keyboard:

•"I do not regret converting to the Simplified Keyboard... as typing on the Old Keyboard had me on the point of resigning from typing. I would advise other typists to convert to this easy method, and not be a mere typist but a Champion or an Expert."

•"I am definitely in favor of the Simplified Keyboard. It does not seem possible that after only six weeks of training I would be typing 57 to 62 WPM in comparison to typing 45 to

50 WPM on the Standard Keyboard after a four year typing course. I certainly would advise other typists to retrain."

•"I do not regret that I have converted, although I was very competent on the Standard keyboard."

•A supervisor of one typist wrote "If it were only the value to the trainees themselves in the pride of acquiring new and progressive skill and the revivifying interest in things official, I would deem the course highly beneficial. If to this be added the overcoming of fatigue, permitting a steady and dependable increase in production throughout the day, there can be no doubt of the advantages of the course to both trainee and employee. I would be glad if I might have the opportunity of offering to all the clerks in my unit the privileges of the course." The man certainly wrote like a bureaucrat, but he had the right idea!

The report's conclusion: "Since these typists had only 83 hours of instruction on the Simplified Keyboard... it is believed that training of beginning typists and retraining of typists whose skill is mediocre or poor is a practical solution to the present shortage of competent typists."

In a follow-up experiment completed later that year (October, 1944), the Navy gave Standard Keyboard training to 18 other typists to see if they could get results comparable to the increase in speed and production the Simplified Keyboard typists made. After an average of 157.6 hours of Standard Keyboard training, their NWPM rate went up by only 8.1 words. (After only 83 hours of training on the Simplified Keyboard, the first group's increase was 24.2 NWPM over their Standard Keyboard rates.)

In addition to the Qwerty group's poor improvement rate, it was calculated that the training cost on the Qwerty keyboard would take 102 to 116 days to be amortized (versus 10.3 days for retraining on the Simplified Keyboard). During that era, the Navy was holding regular "refresher" training classes for its typists in an effort to get typing skill up. This report pointed out how poor the cost-effectiveness of those periodic practice sessions were, especially when compared to the results of the Dvorak retraining.

The follow-up report was even more in support of the switch to the Simplified Keyboard than the original report. Its conclusion said, in part:

> "A tenable program of retraining of the poorer 50 to 60 percent of the Navy Department typists could be accomplished rapidly and smoothly by training pilot individuals or groups from each large office or section in each Bureau and Division. These might well be the poorest typists in each office in order that the temporary loss of their production during the retraining period would cause a minimum of disruption. When retrained, these first Simplified Keyboard typists could, because of their greatly improved skill, temporarily release the next poorer typists for retraining, etc. When all Navy Department typists, regardless of keyboard used, were capable of typing at 70 to 75 NWPM, the program could advisably be discontinued or continued on a much reduced basis. Since the Simplified Keyboard retraining program will amortize itself with each typist in money cost and in typing production within a few weeks, and thereafter will show 75 to 100 percent money and production dividends, and since the retraining meets with the hearty approval

of the typists who   through experience with the Simplified Keyboard have a valid basis for an opinion regarding it, there seem to be no insurmountable obstacles to its immediate initiation."

The Navy's own objective researchers suggested an immediate switch to the Dvorak keyboard in 1944. With the conclusions from these scientific studies, the Navy ordered 2,000 Dvorak typewriters.   But the Treasury Department vetoed the purchase and, shortly afterward, the Navy reports were *classified*. The reports remained classified for several years until the Navy lifted the "accidental" security restriction. But the result was clear: no Dvorak typewriters. It is still not known to the public why the change was not made.

Chapter Five

Why Dvorak isn't the Standard Today

"The typewriter companies and the secretarial schools don't want an increase in productivity. They don't want an office to get the same work out of two typists that used to take three." — Ralph Nader.

If the Dvorak layout is so good, why hasn't it already become the primary keyboard? Dvorak himself was optimistic that his design would eventually catch on, but he didn't expect it to happen overnight.

"It took 35 to 70 years for the railroads, steamships, radio, telephone, telegraph, airplanes, and yes, even the automobile to gain general acceptance after they were invented and/or developed," Dvorak said. Each required "investment of time, money, and effort. (And) each was opposed by those who had investments in the status quo." Today, there are many who are heavily invested in the Qwerty layout, and that's probably the number one reason that a widespread change hasn't been made yet.

But more than the simple cost of conversion has stood in the way. The new keyboard was introduced at a bad time in history, and Dvorak himself made some poor business decisions that hampered the conversion process. Other factors also stood in the way, but as time goes by objections are fading away and the business world is starting to see the advantages of switching.

The Depression

Some of the factors that have stood in the way of Dvorak are quite understandable. Dvorak and Dealey introduced their design at a time when the physical mechanisms of typewriters could handle faster typing (the slow mechanical action of the first typewriters was the design factor most responsible for the Qwerty layout to begin with). But the Simplified Keyboard was presented to the public during the Great Depression of the '30s, a time when businesses didn't have the money to invest in productivity or much else. Conversion of typewriters, which had only recently become a useful business tool, was a low priority item.

If it wasn't feasible to change existing equipment, then perhaps a better approach would be to make the keyboard available on new equipment. But the typewriter companies, like most everyone else, were in dire financial straits. It was bad enough to have sales of their machines slowed as a result of the depressed economy; they didn't need to start making possibly risky investments in a completely new keyboard, which at that time had little objective testing done on it. Dvorak himself didn't help matters when he showed how much more efficient his keyboard made typing; when he came on the scene saying things like "you can do twice the work that you could on your old machine," the typewriter companies took it as "you can get away with buying half the typewriters you are now." So the typewriter companies were reluctant to promote an improvement that might slow typewriter sales even more.

But even with those negative reactions, many in the early 1940s saw the benefit of an easier to learn, less fatiguing layout. Several typewriter companies did begin to offer the Dvorak layout as an option to show that they were keeping up with the times. The new keyboard did, after all, get a great deal of impressive press coverage when it was first introduced. Then, Dr. Dvorak made a fatal business decision: he invested heavily in a new Remington machine, the "Noiseless" typewriter, with the simplified layout as standard. Unfortunately, typists didn't like the "dull thud" sound that the "Noiseless" made, and the typewriter failed in the marketplace. That failure was costly – the doctor lost money and his keyboard lost favor.

World War II

The Dvorak keyboard was down, but not out – until the war started. With hardware needed for the war effort, typewriter manufacturing plants were converted to small arms production, cancelling all manufacturing of new typewriters. Dvorak's Simplified Keyboard was doomed. The War Department issued hundreds of typewriters and to keep them all the same, they converted them all to the most common layout: Qwerty. After the war was over and typewriters went back into production, Qwerty was firmly established as the *de facto* standard.

Even the highly favorable Navy study in 1944 (see Chapter 4) wasn't enough to buck the Qwerty trend. At that time, there were more than 800,000 typewriters in use by the government. It was reasoned that to convert all of those typewriters, at a cost estimated to be $25 each, would cost $20 million and, if for some reason the new keyboard didn't work out or catch on, it would cost another $20 million to change them all back. Why risk $40 million? It was unfortunate reasoning, because the change would have saved many times that amount in productivity in very little time. Apparently the simple solution of experimenting with changeover of small sections of the government at a time wasn't thought of.

The GSA Report

Despite these obstacles, the Dvorak kept bouncing back. There were always people who were convinced that the Dvorak was great, and they were always trying to get others to convert. So in 1956 the government ordered another study. The General Services Administration commissioned Dr. Earl P. Strong of the Pennsylvania State University to conduct a comparison study of the Dvorak and Qwerty layouts.

Twenty typists were recruited from various Federal agencies. Ten, chosen at random, were retrained on Dvorak until their speeds matched their previous Qwerty speed. However, their training time during this phase was four hours per day – much longer than recommended by earlier studies which showed that more than two hours of typing training per day is counterproductive. After the first ten typists were retrained, they were given more training designed to increase their speed and accuracy. At the same time ten Qwerty keyboard typists were given similar training to increase their speed and accuracy.

At the end of the training, the Dvorak group incresased their speed by 27 percent and reduced their error rate by 54 percent in a five minute test. The Qwerty group increased their speed 32 percent, but at the same time their errors increased by 12 percent (also in a five minute test), indicating that the typists were trying to type faster than they were really able.

The final conclusion of the report stated "a recommendation for the adoption of the Simplified Keyboard for use by the Federal Government cannot be justified based on the findings of this experiment." That conclusion, however, was *clearly not supported by the data* published in the report.

Richard Land, a Research Associate in Engineering at Harvard University, called the GSA report "a lesson in how to defeat progress." He wrote that the GSA test was "poorly designed" and that "the conclusions are overstated." He said that even though the simplified keyboard operators were not given enough time to reach their potential competence, they showed "great promise" that was ignored by the experimenters.

Land criticized the experiment for its "limited scope" and said that despite the negative conclusion made by Dr. Strong, the data included in the report showed a significant difference between the keyboards when consideration is made for the test duration.

After the GSA test results were made public, several researchers who noted the inconsistency between the limited data published with the report and the report's conclusion wanted to view the complete, raw data from the experiment in order to make their own conclusions. However, *Dr. Strong had destroyed the data from the experiment*, all except for one film clip that he saved "for a souvenir". Scientific experiments are not generally considered valid if the results cannot be replicated independently by other researchers, but that is not possible when the data and methods of an experiment have been destroyed. Competent researchers make their data and methods available to other researchers.

Other records show that Dr. Strong may not have been the ideal, unbiased researcher he should have been to conduct such an experiment. In 1949, he had written "I have developed a great deal of material on how to get this increased production on the part of typists on the standard keyboard. Consequently, I am not in favor of purchasing new keyboards and retraining typists on the new keyboard. ...I strongly feel that the present keyboard has not been fully exploited, and I am out to exploit it to its very utmost in opposition to the change to new keyboards." Other writings have indicated that Dr. Dvorak and Dr. Strong, who were acquainted long before the GSA experiment, had a strained business relationship.

So if Strong had such a bias against the Dvorak layout from the beginning, why did the government hire him? Because, observers now assume, he was a well-known figure in the world of typewriting research, and the GSA didn't consider the possibility that someone might have a subjective bias against changing away from Qwerty.

Mass Conversion

Many of the objections to conversion cited the high cost of refitting or replacing typewriters. But no one in the Dvorak movement ever advocated changing every typewriter at the same time. Typewriters wear out, typists retire; many feel this is when changes should start.

So, should today's businesses supply their typists with Qwerty or Dvorak typewriters? Should they have both, which might be cost prohibitive? If they stock just one layout, and they hire someone that only knows the other, should they buy equipment to accommodate the new employee or compel the employee to retrain?

Such questions are not trivial for small businesses who cannot afford to have more than one set of typewriters, or for large businesses who don't want to have hundreds of each. But, with electronic typewriters and word processors, such questions become moot.

Typing equipment controlled by computer – such as word processors and personal computers running word processing software – is remarkably easy to convert to Dvorak. In fact, many word processors on the market today have *both* keyboards already built in. If a business has a typist that only knows the Qwerty layout, the typist can push a few keys and the machine will automatically switch from Dvorak to the Qwerty keyboard. (See the appendix for a list of machines already offering this type of feature.)

Dedicated word processors (machines that perform only word processing, and are not programmable for other computerized tasks) have been giving way lately to personal computers. Personal Computers can be loaded with word processing software to take care of that function, but they can also be programmed to do data processing, communications with other computers, and many other tasks that make them more versatile than dedicated word processors.

Even if those machines don't have Dvorak built in, the very nature of their programmability makes them prime Dvorak conversion candidates. Several software packages are available which can quickly and easily convert the keyboard to the Dvorak layout no matter what other software is running on the computer. Many of these programs also have other capabilities, such as the storage of "macro" commands (a series of characters that do complicated functions), the ability to store often-used text (such as common paragraphs, closing lines for a letter, the boss's name, etc.), and other functions.

Several companies make Dvorak replacement keyboards that plug into computers. That way, if more than one operator uses a machine, and they know different layouts, they can plug in the keyboard that matches their skill. Only the keyboard is duplicated, not the entire machine. Some newer replacement keyboards have both layouts internally programmed; a switch selects between them. Some have both Qwerty and Dvorak legends on the key caps.

Now that the Dvorak layout has become a standard recognized by the American National Standards Institute (known better as ANSI), computer manufacturers are building Dvorak capability into their machines. The first such American machine made for mass use was the Apple IIc, the portable version of the popular Apple II computer which helped launch the entire personal computer revolution. The IIc has a switch near the keyboard that permits instant selection of either the Qwerty or the Dvorak layouts. Apple even made a TV commercial showing Barbara Blackburn, the world's fastest typist (she uses the Dvorak on her IIc), typing on her computer at over 200 words per minute.

As more and more products allow a selectable keyboard, the Dvorak is finally catching on for general use. It will become the primary keyboard used in business because of its high productivity, and the primary keyboard used for personal typing because it is easier to learn. Typists like it better because it is easier to use and less tiring. But, with a selectable keyboard, if someone knows only the Qwerty layout, it will still be available for them. And because even inexpensive, small typewriters are increasingly controlled by electronics, the Dvorak will become available on them.

Probably one of the biggest pushes for the Dvorak will come because of the microcomputer revolution, but not for the reason many think. As PCs become a necessary desk fixture for the successful executive and other white collar workers, they will be doing something they haven't had to do before: type. As professionals do more and more of their own keyboarding on their personal computers, they will want to have a typing system that is easier to learn, easier to type on, and more logical than Qwerty, especially if all they can do is "hunt-and-peck". Since secretaries won't be the only ones doing the dirty work of keyboarding anymore, the Dvorak keyboard likely will suddenly become standard equipment on executive's computers.

And even if they do know how to type, the increased productivity of the Dvorak means executives won't be wasting their time – and what executive has time to waste? Best of all, the Dvorak is much faster and easier for them to learn.

Chapter 6

A Program for Conversion

"Where in America today is there a comedy of errors to match contemporary typewriting instruction?" – Dr. August Dvorak.

After much research by experimental psychologists into "what" typewriting really is, most are astounded that we can type at the speeds we do at all. A few years back, *Scientific American* magazine reported that by estimating speeds via psychological testing, typing speeds shouldn't pass about 48 words per minute. Yet there are people who have been able to type more than four times that speed.

Since typewriters have now been around for well over 100 years, some general principles of the teaching of typewriting have been established. Unfortunately, some typing teachers seem to be unaware of many of them. This chapter will aid you in making up your own retraining program. Try to find a manual or computer tutorial that is specifically written for the Dvorak keyboard (see Appendix 1). With the Dvorak, progress is quickly made toward meaningful sentences because the most-used letters are on the home row – the row that is learned first.

Speed

It doesn't take very long to learn where the keys are on a typewriter. The point of training, after the first few days, is to speed up typing to an acceptable level and then bring the error rate down. To do that, training must emphasize hitting the proper key and moving on to the next one as quickly as possible. Slowness and hesitation must be avoided.

At first, when typists are just learning the key positions, they type very slowly. They see or think of the letter to type, think about where the letter is on the keyboard, then think about which finger to move and how to move it.

After some practice, typists become *conditioned* as to where the keys are. They don't have to figure out where each key is or think about what the letter is, they just hit it with a quick stroke. It is at this stage, called "ballistic stroking", where many people stop training; they know where the keys are without looking and without thinking about it. But additional training can bring typing to a higher skill level, giving the typist increased speed and much more accuracy.

Conditioning is a primary psychological concept. Part of that concept is reinforcement. The trainee needs to know how he or she is doing. Therefore, it is important to share test results and to let trainees see what they did right or wrong as soon as possible – preferably immediately.

How fast can typists re-train to Dvorak? It takes much less time than learning how to type in the first place, but don't rush it. Studies show that more than *two hours* of keyboard training per day is a waste, with one hour being a more reasonable figure. And those one or two hours should be broken up with several rest periods. Typists in a retraining program should be able to do non-keyboard work to fill out their day, but they probably should avoid typing. Some trainers, while helping typists to convert, report that typists are reaching their old Qwerty skill in just 18-20 hours of retraining using computer tutorials, then often they move to a higher level of skill with additional training. Generally, though, one hour of retraining time per Qwerty word-per-minute should be allowed (i.e., a 50 WPM Qwerty typist might need up to 50 hours of retraining at two hours or less per day to exceed the 50 WPM barrier).

One of the reasons that the Dvorak is easier to learn when starting from scratch is the ease in stroking the common sequences used in English. On the Qwerty keyboard, the generally weaker left hand does most of the work, and the sequences require complicated finger motions. Those motions must be learned, and their difficulty makes hand conditioning a slow process. Because difficult sequences are virtually eliminated on the Dvorak layout, training is easier.

Also, retraining from Qwerty to Dvorak is easy. One of the hardest things to learn in typewriting is the finger movements, and those movements are used no matter what the keyboard layout is. All that must be learned when retraining is the new location of the keys. So the time spent in learning Qwerty is not, as some have argued, "completely wasted."

Sight Typing

Most beginning typists tend to look at their fingers as they learn. While it isn't efficient to look at the text then at the keyboard then back to the text, not allowing the typist to look at all may create hesitancy. They want to make sure they have the right key before they hit it, so in the beginning stages of training or retraining, sight typing should not be prohibited. Generally, the tendency to look at the keys while typing goes away after the conditioned response sets in.

In fact, some researchers feel sight typing is beneficial. Watching the finger hit the right key is immediate reinforcement – even faster reinforcement than watching the letter appear on the paper or screen. The quicker the reinforcement, the faster the conditioning is learned. If typists watch their fingers, there is more likelihood of the stroke being correct.

Some studies even recommend dictation rather than copying printed material for beginning students to facilitate sight typing. In a group, students type the dictated word or phrase as many times as they can before the next word or phrase is called out. This allows the students to reach their own limits.

Normally, typing students will stop looking at their fingers on their own after several days or weeks of training (depending on their skill levels). If, however, sight typing becomes an undesirable habit, the habit can be broken by forcing the typist to copy material at a rate that does not allow the time to look back and forth.

Studies show that the perception of objects in space (which is where the keyboard is) is easier through vision than feel. So many researchers have concluded that the use of blank or covered keyboards and wall charts only serves to delay the learning process.

Pacing and Rhythm

Rigid timing has been shown to have little value. The practice of "one stroke per second" or the use of a metronome may help typists learn to stroke quickly and evenly at the very beginning stages of training, but after "ballistic" stroking is learned timed pacing is more a hindrance than a help since it disallows the time-efficient "crowding" rhythm (that is, fast, often-used sequences) possible between easy strokes.

It is easier to type rhythmically, but rhythm doesn't mean that there must be even amounts of time between each and every keystroke. Measurements clearly show that the time between strokes is a factor of the difficulty of the particular motion involved. Rigid timing and rhythm requirements can slow the easy sequences and rush the harder ones.

The Dvorak keyboard is especially designed with the idea of easy sequences in mind. Dr. Dvorak consciously reduced the amount of difficult transitions between keys to lessen the time and effort necessary to make them. This ease also reduces the propensity for error, and this reduces the frustration of learning how to type.

After the students learn the keystrokes, it is best to allow each to set their own pace. In a group situation, setting a single pace for the entire class puts undue burden on the slow learners and holds back the fast ones.

Learning the Key Positions

The use of "nonsense words" is one of the worst methods to learn key positions. That is, practice materials consisting of words like "fjf" and "zbsyt" do little to condition keystrokes. It is likely that the use of such word combinations is the fault of the Qwerty layout; there are only about 100 meaningful words on Qwerty's home row (the row learned first, where the fingers normally rest) versus *several thousand* on the Dvorak home row. With that many words available, it is easy to make interesting and meaningful sentences in the first hours of training.

Nonsense words are not only boring and therefore decrease the student's motivation, but they usually consist of letter combinations that *do not exist* in normal typing. There is no reason to condition a sequential response that will never be used while simultaneously ignoring combinations that will be. Also, nonsense words keep the typist at the lowest level of skill: the letter-by-letter level. The typist isn't allowed the necessary opportunity to practice typing at the word, phrase, or sentence level. Finally, it is much more difficult to see where errors occur when the word doesn't mean anything to begin with.

In fact, a government study showed that using nonsense words was ineffective even for training radio operators who only transmitted seemingly meaningless codes. The bottom line is that normal words are best for training typists no matter what kind of work is required.

+Increasing Speed

The ability to learn accuracy and the ability to learn speed are *not* directly related. Of course, if a typist goes faster than he is normally able, the error rate will be quite high. But both slow and fast typists' error rates range between low and high. Speed building and accuracy improvement are different skills; they should not be attempted at the same time.

A substantial portion of a typing training program should consist of speed training. Allowing speed to develop on its own while typing on the job is a waste; it doesn't allow for a concentrated effort to reach the highest possible speed.

The goal of speed building is to speed up of the association between perception of the text to be typed and the movement necessary to strike the keys, and to acquire the conditioned response for typing sequences. Therefore, the typist should work on relatively simple materials and concentrate on typing as fast as is *comfortable* – the way to learn to type faster is to do your best to type faster! The error rate may go up at first, but *errors made during this time should be ignored.* Errors are an indication that speed is indeed increasing and that new methods of finger movements are being tried. Slow motion studies of expert typists clearly show that fast typing is physically different from slow typing. That difference must be learned through practice.

"Comfortable" is stressed because excessive speed often leads to excessive muscle tension in the fingers. Excessive tension inhibits the "ballistic" strokes mentioned earlier.

Next, it is best to practice using a variety of materials. That is, don't keep typing the same sentence or page again and again. It becomes boring, and the typist ends up learning the text more than learning how to type more effectively. Materials should be varied, as well as the time spent on drill sessions, to simulate normal typing behavior.

Increasing Accuracy

Again, most researchers agree that in the early stages of training, errors should be *ignored*. Then, after speed is up, the concentration should switch to accuracy. If error rates are emphasized in the early stages of training, the trainee slows down to be more careful. When this happens, the typist doesn't develop the quick transition from letter to letter that makes typing so fast. Also, studies show that training for accuracy does not carry over into higher speeds, but speed training *is* retained when the emphasis of training switches to accuracy.

Unfortunately, it is difficult if not impossible to give lessons on how to increase accuracy. Not only are there several different types of errors that typists make, but they occur for different reasons. Furthermore, an Air Force study concluded that errors aren't usually the result of a particular poorly learned letter, but "a key is mis-struck because the preceding or following stroke makes the *sequence* difficult to finger."

As has been stressed in earlier chapters, Dr. Dvorak studied sequences intensively in designing his keyboard, so Dvorak error rates are on average *much* lower than Qwerty error rates. This is demonstrated when instructors who teach the Dvorak layout report that students tend to make fewer errors while learning that keyboard. So the Dvorak fits in well with the theory presented in the Air Force report.

While it is hard to say what special things can be done to reduce errors, it is much easier to say what *not* to do. The following have proved *ineffective*:

•High standards of accuracy from the beginning of training

•Repetitive practice on problem words

•Negative practice (the intentional mistyping of problem words)

•Forced pacing drills (such as with a metronome)

•Drills with nonsense words

Typewriter "Demons"

The ten words most frequently mispelled on:

Qwerty	Dvorak
1-the	1-new
2-to	2-beautiful
3-of	3-during
4-and	4-everything
5-is	5-help
6-which	6-oblige
7-it	7-certain
8-that	8-company
9-when	9-length
10-for	10-October

Also in the Qwerty top-100 list: be, in,do,my, as, can, if, I

There are no two-letter words on the Dvorak top 100, and no other three-letter words after "new".

Notice that the words on the Qwerty list are short, simple words that are used every day – the errors aren't due to spelling difficulty, but to the awkward finger motions necessary to type them.

The words on the Dvorak list are much longer and less frequently used, indicating that they are mispelled because they are more difficult words.

"Mental Practice"

One proponent of the Dvorak keyboard suggested that while waiting for their specially ordered typewriter to arrive, Dvorak purchasers get a full-size diagram of the keyboard and practice "typing" on it. Then, when their new typewriter actually arrived, they would already be familiar with it.

Many athletes believe that such mental practice is beneficial in certain physical activities, such as individual sports. It would follow, then, that this type of practice might be beneficial in learning a new keyboard. However, no studies have been made to confirm this.

Beginning students, by the way, tend to be easily overwhelmed by intensive training. In the first few hours of training, it may be beneficial to give the students frequent breaks.

Who Should Retrain?

Ideally, there should be only one keyboard in use today, and if you have read this far, you should agree that the one keyboard should be Dvorak. But what about the employee who has typed on Qwerty for 20 or 30 years, and is firmly against having to chuck that experience for a new layout? Should these people be forced to either change or lose their jobs?

It's a hard question, but if their skill is adequate, why threaten them? With electronically switchable keyboards, these people can be accommodated. Most typists, when told there is a new keyboard on the horizon, are reluctant to switch; they don't want to see their hard-earned talent go to waste. They remember the ordeal of learning how to type in the first place and, understandably, they don't want to go through that again.

Luckily, one of the major factors in learning how to type is learning to coordinate finger motions. That learning is *not* wasted when the keyboard layout is switched; this skill is needed no matter what keyboard is used. Also, due to the logical arrangement of the Dvorak keyboard, it takes much less time to learn than Qwerty did in the first place.

Typically, after reluctantly agreeing to change to the new keyboard, typists are thrilled with their new Dvorak skill. Dvorak typing is easier on the fingers because of the lessened finger travel, and it is less frustrating because fewer errors are made. The author of this book has not talked to one person who, after learning Dvorak, wanted to return to Qwerty typing. Indeed, he has heard of many who participated in experimental studies who demanded to be supplied with a Dvorak typewriter from then on.

A typist's speed is a poor determining factor when deciding whether to retrain. Often, a typist will shy away from Dvorak retraining, asking why they should bother – they are already capable of typing 70, or 80, or 90 words per minute. But the real power of the Dvorak isn't in the increased speed, though many do find that their speed does increase after switching. The main benefit for these typists is the reduced finger travel, making typing less tiring, and the reduced error potential, making typing less frustrating.

Dvorak International Federation president Virginia Russell was asked to speak to a group of court reporters, who are paid by the page. She was surprised to learn that they already typed at 120 WPM. But they didn't care whether they could type faster on the Dvorak; they wanted to get rid of the ache in their hands caused by the excessive hand motion that the Qwerty produces after a long day of typing. They switched, and the aches have gone away. And even though they didn't get their speed up much past their original 120 WPM, their error rates are lower, so their production – and paychecks – are higher.

Faster. Easier to learn. Less tiring. More productive. Pays for itself quickly. It almost sounds too good to be true, but it isn't. In more than 50 years of trials, experiments and studies, the Dvorak has proven itself again and again. Major businesses and governmental agencies *have* started to convert their equipment to Dvorak to get these benefits. Don't be the last one to switch.

Chapter 7

One-Hand Typing

"To require the one-hand amputee or paralytic to master touch typing on the (Qwerty) keyboard is a form of sadistic cruelty reminiscent of the worst in the Middle Ages."
– Dr. August Dvorak

It was in April, 1945 when Colonel Robert Allen lost his right arm while advancing on Germany with General Patton. Allen had been a writer before the war, and it didn't take long before he realized that typing was going to be much more difficult with only one hand.

Dr. Dvorak was still in the Navy at this time, and was in Washington D.C. Allen was in Walter Reed hospital and since he was familiar with Dvorak's simplified keyboard design, he asked Dvorak if he would design an efficient one-hand keyboard for him. Dvorak quickly realized that there would be a need by others for such a keyboard, so he designed two: one for the right hand, one for the left. It was a natural extension of the work Dr. Dvorak had done for typists in general.

Like the original two-hand Dvorak keyboard, the one-hand Dvorak keyboards were designed for maximum efficiency and comfort. Dvorak used the same data he had gathered and the principles that he had developed for his original design, so it took only a short time to design the specialized keyboards.

Ten weeks after he got his one-hand typewriter, Col. Allen was typing on it at 56 WPM, a speed considerably faster than most people on the Qwerty keyboard using two hands! Dr. Dvorak had written a special one-hand typing manual for Col. Allen which was widely copied and distributed to other one-handers, but the manual has long been out of print.

These keyboards are not meant for the average typist, just for those who must make do with one hand. If you have only one hand, or are missing several fingers from one of your hands, you probably know how difficult it is to type on the Qwerty layout. On the one-hand boards, within reach of your single hand, are the 21 keys that make up 97.6 percent of all typing. The other five letters are reached with some difficulty, but with your hand still in the "home" position – your hand doesn't have to jump all over the keyboard.

Just as the "classic" Dvorak layout was modified (mostly, the digits were put back into arithmetic order), the "classic" Dvorak one-hand layouts have been modified. When Smith Corona came out with their stock ASK typewriters in the 1970s, they also made available one-hand typewriters. The keyboard layouts on these machines also had slight variations from Dvorak's original design (again, mostly digit order). The letters (and the period and comma) are still in the same place Dr. Dvorak put them, and they should remain there for maximum efficiency.

The one-handed layouts are not a part of the ANSI standard. In fact, it is very difficult to find any information at all about these special designs. In typewriting, as in many other areas, problems of the handicapped have been generally ignored.

However, one-hand layouts are available on computers. Many of the same keyboard reconfiguration programs listed in Appendix 1 can be used to create the keyboards shown in this chapter.

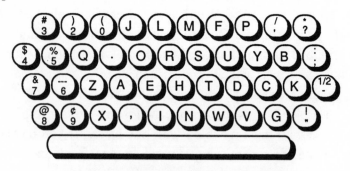

Dvorak's "classic" one-hand keyboard
for the Right hand.

Dvorak's "classic" one-hand keyboard
for the left hand.

Smith-Corona's right-hand keyboard.

Smith-Corona's left-hand keyboard.

Sources

As of press time, these are the companies known to have Dvorak-related products available, the product name, application, cost, and description. Cost and applications change rapidly, so use this information only as a general guide.

As of this writing, there are no known typewriters available with the Dvorak layout, but there should be at least one by the time you read this. The *Dvorak Developments* newsletter (see the listing for **Freelance Communications** below) reports on the products that are currently available.

Many of the computer-related items can be ordered through your computer dealer.

Companies are listed in alphabetical order

Age of Reason, 318 East 6th Street #123, New York NY 10003
"PC/DVORAK"
IBM PCs and compatibles, $30
Software; converts keyboard to Dvorak.

Apple Computer
Apple IIc computer
The Apple IIc has the Dvorak built in on U.S. models.

Arrays, 11223 South Hindry Avenue, Los Angeles CA 90045
"Learn to Type"
Apple IIc, IIe, and Macintosh, IBM PC and compatibles, and Commodore 64, $49.95
Software; typing tutorial for the Dvorak layout.

Camwil, 875 Waimanu Street, Honolulu HI 96813
Elements and wheels for typewriters to convert them to Dvorak. $65-85

Command Software, 1360 N. Main Street, Walnut Creek CA 94596
"Command Writer"
IBM PC and compatibles, $150
Software; word processing program which has an option to re-map the keyboard to Dvorak.

Digital Equipment Corp.
All terminals and computers – Dvorak layout optional.

Dvorak International Federation, PO Box 128, Brandon
VT 05733, (802) 247-6020
Informational agency
Offers memberships for telephone consultation, also stocks
several products for immediate shipment, including Dvorak
typing manuals.

Faultline Micro, PO Box 3147, Fullerton CA 92634
Conversion package
Apple IIe computer, $39.95
Hardware; allows selection of Dvorak at any time.

Freelance Communications, PO Box 717, Arcata CA 95521
Publishes Dvorak Developments, a newsletter about the Dvorak.
Published this book, also stocks other publications about the
Dvorak.

Hooleon Company, PO Box 201, Cornville AZ 86325
Keyboard overlays
Many computers and terminals supported, $26.95
Stickers to place on keyboard keytops to show the layout of
Qwerty and Dvorak so that both kinds of typists can use the
machine.

Kea Systems, 2150 West Broadway Suite 412, Vancouver BC
CANADA, V6K 4L9
"ZSTEMpc-4014 and -VT100"
IBM PC and compatibles, $99-150 US
Software; allows PC to mimic special computer terminals,
Dvorak mapping of the keyboard is supported.

Key Tronic, PO Box 14687, Spokane WA 99214
Computer keyboards with Dvorak layout
IBM PC and compatibles, $209-255; IBM PCjr, $219-255
Hardware; plug-compatible keyboards for instant conversion to
Dvorak.

Maxi-Switch, 9697 NW East River Road, Coon Rapids MN
55433
Computer keyboards with Dvorak layout
IBM PC and compatibles, $125
Hardware; plug-compatible keyboards for instant conversion to
Dvorak.

Mindscape, 3444 Dundee Road, Northbrook IL 60062
"Keyboard Cadet"
Apple II series, IBM PC and compatibles, Commodore 64,
$39.95
Software; typing tutorial for the Dvorak keyboard.

Paragon Courseware, 4954 Sun Valley Road, Del Mar CA
92014
"MacQwerty"
Apple Macintosh, $35
Software; reconfigures keyboard to any layout, Dvorak
definition file included.

Power Up!, PO Box 306, Half Moon Bay CA 94019
"Keyboard Master"
IBM PCs and compatibles, $49.95
Software; typing tutorial for the Dvorak layout.

Prelco, 14202 Galy Street, Tustin CA 92680
"Dv Typer"
Commodore 64 and 128, $36.95
Software; typing tutorial for the Dvorak, supplied with
keyboard overlays to show the key positions and Conversion
package.
-also from Prelco:
Replacement keyboard ROM
Commodore 64, $39.95
Hardware; allows selection of Dvorak at any time.

Q.A.D. Systems, 342 East Schrock Road, Westerville OH
43081
"Q-Vert Mentor"
Commodore 64, $29.95
Software; Dvorak keyboard tutorial program.

QED Information Sciences, PO Box 151, Wellesley MA
02181
"Typing Made Easy"
IBM PC and compatibles, Apple IIc series, Apple Macintosh,
$59.95
Software; typing tutorial for the Dvorak layout.

Rosesoft, 4710 University NE #601, Seattle WA 98105
"Prokey"
IBM PC and compatibles, $129.95
Software; allows keyboard to be programmed (including
macros), includes a file to convert to Dvorak layout. A file to
convert to the one-hand Dvorak layouts is available on request.

Scarborough Systems, 55 South Broadway, Tarrytown NY
10591
"MasterType"
Apple II series, $39.95
Software; typing tutorial. MasterType is available for several
different machines, but only the Apple version supports the
Dvorak keyboard.

Seasoned Systems, PO Box 3720, Chapel Hill NC 27514
"SureStroke/Dvorak"
IBM PC and compatibles, $95
Software; converts keyboard to Dvorak, and includes Dvorak
typing tutorial program and keytop overlays.

Sierra On-Line, PO Box 485, Coarsegold CA 93614
"WizType"
Apple II series, $34.95 Commodore 64, $24.95
Software; Dvorak typing tutorial.

Software Research Technologies, 3757 Wilshire Blvd
Suite 211, Los Angeles CA 90010
"SmartKey"
Most CP/M and MS-DOS computers supported, $49.95
Software; allows keyboard to be programmed, includes a file to
convert to Dvorak layout.

Southern California Research Group, PO Box 593,
Moorpark CA 93021
"The Magic Keyboard"
Apple II and II+, $49.95
Hardware; allows selection of regular Dvorak and one-hand
Dvorak layouts.

Switch to Dvorak, PO Box 2919, Satellite Beach FL 32937
Conversion package
Apple IIe computer, $25
Hardware; allows selection of Dvorak at any time.

Upstart Publishing, PO Box 22022, Greensboro NC 27420
"/SPEEDPACK/"
Commodore 64 and 128, $15
Software; companion product for word processors to convert
them to Dvorak other Dvorak products in the works.

Roger Wagner Publishing, PO Box 582, Santee CA 92071
"The Write Choice"
Apple II series, $44.95
Software; word processor and typing tutor. The tutorial
includes lessons for Dvorak typing.

Wico, 6400 Gross Point Road, Niles IL 60648
"SmartBoard"
IBM PC and compatibles, $399 Apple II line, $399 plus optional
adapter.
Hardware; plug-compatible keyboard for instant conversion to
Dvorak.

Xpert Software, 8865 Polland Avenue, San Diego CA 92123
"XtraKey"
Many computers with CP/M 2.2 operating system supported,
$39.95
Software; allows keyboard to be programmed, includes a file to
convert to Dvorak layout.

Dedicated Word Processors

Many word processors have the capability to set the keyboard up with a Dvorak layout. Those machines include:

CPT
Digital Equipment's DECMATE
Hewlett Packard's 2626W
IBM Displaywriter
Vydec's 1800
Wang OIS and VP

Diagrams

The main diagrams from the book for side-by-side comparison.

The standard Dvorak keyboard as
approved by ANSI.

The standard Qwerty keyboard as
approved by ANSI.

The original Qwerty keyboard from
the Remington Model 1 typewriter.

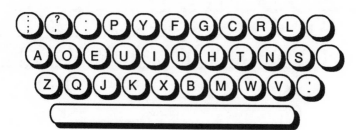

The first Dvorak Simplified Keyboard,
as shown from the patent specification.

Dvorak's "classic" Simplified Keyboard,
as shown in *Typewriting Behavior*.

Smith-Corona's "ASK" or
American Simplified Keyboard.

Dvorak "classic" keyboard
for the right hand.

Dvorak "classic" keyboard
for the left hand.

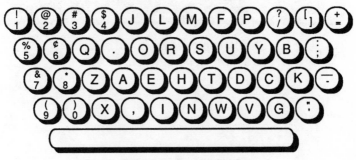

Smith-Corona's Dvorak keyboard
for the right hand.

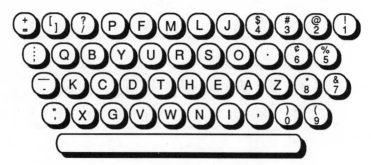

Smith-Corona's Dvorak keyboard
for the left hand.

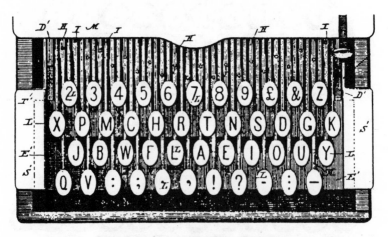

Sholes' improved keyboard design,
as shown on his patent application.

Glossary

Alternate keyboard: the official designation of the Dvorak by the American National Standards Institute.

American National Standards Institute (ANSI): a group of manufacturers which standardizes designs, processes and proceedures to simplify the manufacturing process. They do not endorse any particular process or require that products meet their standards.

American Simplified Keyboard (ASK): a variant of the Dvorak keyboard introduced nt the Smith-Corona typewriter company in 1975.

"Ballistic" stroking: a level of skill where the key to be struck is hit quickly without conscious thought about what its location is.

Classic Dvorak: Dvorak's ideal keyboard, recognizable by its unique number order.

Demon: a word that is particularily difficult to type, and thus is prone to be miskeyed. The determining factor is often the structure of the keyboard – not the structure of the word.

Ergonomics: the study of the interaction between humans and machines and the effort to make human/machine interaction more comfortable and productive.

Finger load: the relative amount of work a finger must do (i.e., the percentage of strokes assigned to each finger by the design of the keyboard.

Finger travel: the amount of distance the fingers must travel over the keyboard. Finger travel is a good indication of the relative efficiency of a particular keyboard design.

Net words per minute (NWPM): a typing speed measurement. The gross speed minus a penalty for errors, usually 5-10 WPM per error.

Qwerty ("kuh-WHERE-tee"): the traditional keyboard layout found on most typewriters and computers.

Simplified keyboard: any variant of the Dvorak keyboard – now usually refers to the "classic" Dvorak design.

Index

Did You Borrow This Book?

Get Your Own!

__ Yes, send *The Dvorak Keyboard* for $12.95 each.

__ Let me know about what other Dvorak-related publications are available.

Enclosed for ___ copies of *The Dvorak Keyboard*, is

      _____ ($12.95 each)

      _____ (plus 6% Sales Tax if shipped to Calif.)

      1.00 ___ (Shipping)

      _____ **Total**

Send this form to:

Freelance Communications

NOTE OUR NEW ADDRESS:

Post Office Box 1895
Upland, CA 91785